POISE &
ARROWS

ISBN 978-1-9992558-0-0

Front cover art and internal book formatting by Nikiya at Grey Ritual Studios in Montreal, Kimberley Castlemain and Mathew MacQuarrie, La.

Dear Reader,

I named this book *Poise and Arrows* — because it's one of my favourite lines of poetry in this collection. The poem that contains this line was written about a feeling of deep regret I couldn't put my finger on. Whatever it was, it had cost me all my poise as a woman, something I learned too late that I truly valued and had taken for granted. Hard times and bad decisions had robbed me of it all. As a result, I felt lost, and I suppose the arrow reference is me simply looking for the way.

This is not really how I write poetry though: in a logical way that expresses my feelings in cute stories that rhyme. In reality, the feelings come first, in droves. Hard. And I let myself feel them. I let my brain do what it wants, which is to indulge in dramatics. Woe is me. After that it actually comes out quite effortlessly. It pours onto the paper much faster than I can possibly understand it. It's only when I come back to a poem some days or weeks later that I make sense of it. Furthermore, I only tend to unpack my poems like I have just done, when I am talking to someone who is interested in how or why I write. Those people are kind of rare. Perhaps you are one of them. For the record, the answer is because I have to, and so I do. It's a beautiful, blessed thing.

Then there's the old play on words: Poise and Arrows? Or *Poison Arrows*? I do love a good play on words. I like to twist things, switch them out to trick you. Sneaky puns. Poison arrows are little shots I take at things and people that upset me. I've definitely turned the bow on myself from time to time and I have a pocket full of prose to prove it.

Poise and Arrows is also a phrase that points to a duality. If we think about arrows in the sense of weapons, would someone with poise shoot arrows? Had I shot my poise with an arrow? Either way, there's a lot of duality in this book. Heaven, hell, angels, demons, love, hate, joy, regrets, chaos, order . . . there are many common themes and sometimes two or more poems might be very similar, as if they were part of a wider story my subconscious is trying to untangle.

I started writing poems and lyrics in December 2016, consequently after I started meditating for the first time in my 29 years. I don't think I can separate these two occurences for cause and effect, which I find utterly fascinating. One day I could not write poetry or meditate. The next I could do both. And it's as if I had unlocked something. As if an eternal tap was suddenly turned on, destined to run forever. I have not stopped writing or meditating since. Meditation is now my own version of Steven Pressfield's prayer to the Muse. I'm endlessly grateful that both things have become permanent strongholds in my life.

The most wonderful thing about deciding to publish a book of poetry was going back through all of it, over a thousand pages, to carry out the curation process. I could actually *see* my writing improve over time. I started to see those trends and themes and understand my writing style, perhaps even myself a little more too. Over the course of those two years, there were times I sat down and rewrote many of them by hand (I write *everything* in my iPhone Notes app, or on the same app on my MacBook). Writing them out by hand helped me to reconnect with them, and never failed to re-inspire me if, for example, I felt I had not written anything earth-shattering for a while. It happens. I return to the source. And all is well.

I left out a lot of poems that came out as lyrics. To me, that means they emerged in song structure/format. When a certain paragraph sounds as if it were born to be a chorus, or certain lines in a sequence read like a pre-chorus hook building to a crescendo. If you want to hear what these poems would sound like if they were music, you can. I worked with a talented first-time producer to record two of my pieces as songs, and they were released in 2018 under the artist name *Baby Grand*. Like the piano. It was an exhilarating experience that gave me a sonic representation of what you'll read here. Grazie Pasquale.

Before I go on forever . . . I want to call out some other important people in this journey. Anyone who has spoken to or interacted with me in any way, shape or form over the past two years, know that I cannot assure you that there aren't poems in this book that are about you. I don't know whether to thank you, or apologize to you. Words can be knives. But they can also be kisses. Choose your own adventure, my friends.

Joe Bagel: I have to call you out personally. Last winter I attended your play at the Diving Bell theatre in Montreal. I have the printed copy of that playbook by my front door next to where I place my keys every single day. When I look at that book, I think *'Man, that guy didn't ask for permission to write a play and put it on! He just did it!'* It was his first play. Half the cast were not even real actors (including himself) and they were all reading from a printed script. He was nervous beforehand, and encouraged the audience to grab their copy of the book to follow along, and don't forget to redeem your free shot downstairs at the Blue Dog during intermission! Or now! Or two!

Joe just did it. Was it perfect? No. Was it the most interesting and unique event I had been to in forever? Absolutely. What I loved most was the balls of it. He didn't wait for permission from himself or anyone else. He just did it. And, honestly, it pushed me over the edge. I realized there was absolutely nothing stopping me from creating something of my own, and giving it to the world. The result of that realization is what you now hold in your hands.

I also want to call out Mathew MacQuarrie. He said the darndest thing to me one day. I was telling him I wanted *so* badly to be a songwriter. It was my dream. I idolized people who could do that for a living. He simply replied — *you are a songwriter.* I can't explain how much that meant to me. Thank you for supporting me, believing in me and for carefully reading my poems every time I shoved one in your face. You have the patience of a saint. You are my muse, and my absolute favourite person ever.

Please take a bite out of my soul, which has been turned inside out to feel the things I felt in order to write these poems. Please do that thing where you give the book to your best book friend once you've finished reading it, then miss how it makes you feel and procure another one. Or don't. I just hope that this touches *someone* I don't know personally, outside of my six degrees of separation. That would be magical. And I do believe in magic. I hope you find your poise and arrows in these pages. I certainly found mine.

Kim

The Voice

It's honey in your hands
Sugar down your spine
You crumble like a cigarette
You're wasted from no wine

Would you believe
That a single tune
Could be heard
From the Heavens
And melted the moon
Clouds turned to dust
And the stars they were weeping
This was the sound
That woke angels sleeping

For Lea

Her Religion

She said she could see
The things in the painting moving
And I wanted to have eyes like hers

I wanted her lips
But more than that
I wanted to see
How her lips might move
When her eyes
Saw something beautiful

I'm open to things
That send a chill down my spine
A forgotten freckle
A watery wine

Things that will never be the same
A chip in a gilded picture frame
A glossy ash on the mirror
Where you brush your hair
Staring through yourself
Wishing I was there

Peeling back the layers
Of lies you packed on
To shut me out
Like the wall around your heart

I look at you the same way
Like the way she looks at art
It's her religion
She has faith in you
So what are you going to do?

Make me sorry I ever met you
Make me sorry

Castle Closed for the Ever

Like broken clockwork
There you are before me
Again
Taking my hands

In a pattern I can't predict
Because our castle
Was only built from sand

And nobody lives there now
Rapunzel sold her locks for cash
And skipped town

Roadmap of Ruins

Everywhere I look
I'm falling like an angel
Followed by devils
Straight out of God's good book

But the bible cannot tell me
What kind of hell
They're trying to sell me
And I wonder if I'll ever get back
The things you took

So if not evil or good
How do I know if it's right?
To love this other one
Who doesn't look at all
Like he should?

He's not like the others
Not like any many I've ever known
And he's not mine
But I love him more than anything
I could ever own
Anyway

An ode to going off the rails
To survive a longing
That hurts like the heavens
And heals like a holy hymn

A painstaking pleasure
You would live and die through
Just to feel the sweat of a sorry sin

But it isn't sweet
This unmade bed of nails
Lets no sinners sleep

Edge Curse

What would you do
If I just turned right around
And fell for you?

I could just let go
You might never know...

Are we going to do this dance,
Or what?
Will you ever voice
What I know to be true,
Or not?

We could be like
Sand in a honey jar
Making wings out of worries
In the summer
Climbing up on stars

But I know this much
I'll never give in... first.

A Place Called Poise

Lead me through the lies
And tether me to the truth
I can't float around forever
In this nebulous abuse

The smoke looks in the mirror
And they laugh
About being cliche
Together

And in the looking glass
I'll find a way to fade
I'll do it fast
It'll be forever

Because if I hold my arms open
Any longer
You'll likely rip them off
Just to tear out my heart

And then you'll take my eyes
Cos you wanna hurt me
And then not allow me
The leisure of crying

If dignity was a bone
In the body
Where would it fit?

If poise was a place

Somewhere

Would I be able to

Run away to it?

Winter Wisdom

As the temperature dips just below
And we get the first hints of snow
I feel complete
I feel at ease
Even as my fingers freeze

Because at least now
There are friends in the fight
In the loneliness of what went wrong
My winter clothes will hold me tight

I carry around these layers
Like the questions and regrets
Every minute
Each one circles my mind
At least twice

They get in the way
I slip and fall - it isn't nice
They hide behind
The glitter of snowflakes
Over the snide black ice

While it's cold
And the season puts on
It's best show
I'll keep warm
And think about
How I can't accept it
Can't change it
And can't let it go

Heart Home

You broke my heart open
And I was real
Like clouds that are white
And words that are spoken

You came inside
And made a home there
So I would know you tried

You would stay a while
You'd take your time
And walk a million miles
To bring me back

Now you come to me with words
With a distant hand
I see you in my dreams
And I'll never understand

This world
Full of feelings and faults
I used to see stars
I will miss them the most

Blue Eyes i

Been fired from every job
You ever had
They call you horrible
But you're not so bad

You're a thing
I want to keep
When I'm tired
You're the deepest sleep

You're worth fixing everything for
I want to be the window
When you can't find the door

You're the one who kissed me
The one I got
When I thought I had everything
But there was more

You're the one I waited for
The one I needed
To know I could win the fight
And settle my own score

For a while we danced in circles
And you ran
Until you couldn't anymore
We laid down on the floor
Together

You understand me
It is this I adore
You make me better

Baby, blue eyes
Are the best thing you ever wore

Sorry Surrender

At least this time
I saw it coming
Before it swallowed me whole

But that didn't stop me
From laying down
And taking it all

The violent caress
Of a falling fever
The wedding dress
Floating down the river

I've been to the other side
And back
Now I'm coloured blue
And red and black

But I saw what was coming
And I layed right down
I let it take me

Maybe someday it'll bring me
Back around…

Slow for Show

I let you be too much
I let myself be soft
And grew too fond of your touch

And now I need it more
Than anything
But something stops me short

I'm kept at arm's length
Cos you wanna take it slow
But you look into my eyes
And it's like you know
What you really want
But you're scared as hell
Babe don't you know
I'm scared as well?

Sail the Teas

A sunny day that turns to rain
A smile that fades to the look of pain
The sounds that once held excitement close
A promising life and an overdose

Come walk in my shoes
And see how I live
Take everything
That I've got to give

Because I'm running
Out of time
And tea
I'm trying to sail
All seven seas
At once
It's a hearty task
And time
She goes fast

Trust v World

Maybe it's your word against theirs
But it's all the same

For all I know
All I really know is true about you
Is your name

I'm not your girl
And it's the notion of trust
Versus everyone in the world

You love to recall
The very first thing
I ever said to you at all

It's a voice for the ages
And a heavy breath
Like I've never heard
It's the perfect entanglement
Of our limbs
And how much is said
Without a single word
You pull me in
And I'm already ready
For us to begin

Rain and Regrets

My cigarette is stained
With a blushing rouge
The mark upon the lips
I kissed you with
Yesterday

As I think about
What I did
What I should have done
And what I did not do
I walk in the starting rain
And I think of you

Lonely Lane

You promised her you'd never do it
But I swear you did
Just like I did too

And it's a cruel set of facts
We take down so deep
Like a pill of pain
An unrestful sleep

Pain is more than a feeling
It's a place I live
While I wait for you

And loneliness is more
Than a longing
It's the lane I live on

Mile End

How to not think
And yet know a thing all the same
How to trick your mind
Into losing at its own favourite game

A respite from the ruin
Of your own favourite place
Alone in lonely rooms
Where mirrors hide
Your unfamiliar face

At the end of the mile
Everything is temporary
But you can find a smile
Around any corner
A peaceful place
In a borrowed border

Passing Crime

I won't go to bed
With your song stuck in my head
I'll write another verse
To cry and break the curse

I'll pour another drink
Because the past is pink
And the future is blue
I'll take a walk around the block
And think of you

The Paper Promise

You feel like an imminent pain
Grey and hurtful like that night
I walked home in the pouring rain

Feel like I know it's coming
I always did
And it's anything but sweet

I almost want to see you with her
Secretly . . . walking down the street

Cos I want a reason to know
I need to be pushed
Something to make me let go

You make my heart race my dear
But not with excitement - f e a r

//

You feel like soft satin safety
Comfortable like a place
I can rest my head

With you I never have to worry
Never have to wonder
What you meant
By what you said

Feel like I know it's coming
A time where
It's us against the world

Like we cracked the code
We found the secret
To lovers growing old

You remind me of who I am
When I forget
You help me find my center
And you show me respect

My heart is racing
In the best kind of way
I think I made a decision t o d a y

Always Wear Black

Cornflour clouds
And a well full of wishes
I wish I could wash out
My heart with the dishes

The time that it takes
Just to float up that high
Take your sweet time
As the clouds float on by

Whatever happens
I'll be by your side
I'm your sweet sidekick
Along for the ride
And if we should falter
I'll carry us back
Promise me baby
You'll always wear black

You wanna move forward
So don't go back
Promise me baby
You'll always wear black

No Time for Identity

Don't have a story to carry around
Just be here with me now
Don't tell a tale of time, my friend
Just be, and breathe somehow

We hold onto our vices
Our names, and all we think we are
We look forward to the future
And look back to see how far

The moment here is fleeting
Full of love and life and light
But we dance around the day we're in
It's an awful, tiresome fight

Laps of Life

Let there be just enough hesitation
For you to make
All the best decisions

When you're scared and unsure
Let your gut do all the long divisions
Of life

Let there be stars in your eyes
And hope in your heart

May you always find the courage you need
To just start
Again

Steal the Sun

I was walking
The sun stood strong
And I smiled
Like I hadn't in so long

I was filled
With something hard to find
Because the night you kissed me first
Was on my mind

You say you feel it too
And you make out
Like I'm the only one
You say there's something here
And you make me want
To steal the sun
And paint the sky
Because you made me fall in love with you
That's why

Body v Soul

Oh biology
How are you, you
And I me?

Where do we two divide?
And how are we each
Supposed to 'be'?

Seeds for my Sorry Soul

My heart had become a Death Valley
A desolate place
You moved in and grew a garden
Where you saw there was space
I didn't see

And this garden
Grew in me
I blossomed
Like a springtime sun
Was shining all for me

I can smile now
And I can even stand crying
If that's what it takes
To keep my plants and flowers
From dying

If the tears are what's needed
To keep the soil from drying
Now that my heart has been seeded
I even feel like trying

You helped me see
I could be a garden
And I could be free

Lonely? Leave.

Met a fireman in New York
When my jeans didn't hug me
Like they did before

Took a bus across the state line
Because I felt lonely
And you needed time

Now when I look up
The sky is changing
With the seasons
And you tell me
You have your reasons

But as you drift away
So do all the memories
Of our summer days

And I forget just how
We got here at all
But I won't forget the feeling
When I took the fall

Cos it was all too much
I'd shake and babe
I couldn't breathe
Until I felt your touch

Needed to have you there
Needed too much

And though you tried
You couldn't care
Enough for me
So now I see

With shaking arms
From the weight of this
Heavy heart
I'll drag us away
And find a brand new start

Fighting the Unrequited

Touch the light as it shines
Draw a line
In the sands of time

Be the desert divide
Be the one they look for
And come calling
Far and wide

Make a place that doesn't exist
Be the face, upon which
We find the lips
We can never kiss

O Goodbye Heart

Back to the beginning
In more ways than one
Trying to uplift
While coming undone

To go through the motions
Is motion at least
Finding my way
Making my peace

Forego resistance
Give up desire
Take a sweet step
Build an empire

Hold up your heart
It won't fly away
It only gets easier
Lighter each day

Your heart is a haven
I wanted to stay
But I'm climbing out
I'm running away

Madness or Music

I've been drinking and smoking
Crying and coping

One day I'm on fire
The next caught up
Broken and empty
Feeling too much

I can't sit still
Without unruly aching
I can't get over
My heart is breaking

I'm lost and unsure
Scared and confused
I've never felt more foolish
Never more used

But life is a game
And we all play to win
We got what we wanted
The fire, the sin

But after the fire
While fanning the flames
I hadn't caught on
To the sick little games

Blinded by something
I wanted to see
There's no tale of us
There's no "you and me"

Maybe there was
But it's over now
I'll crawl through the cut glass
I'll howl at the sound

The sound will hurt less
As it turns into music
I'm finding my voice
And I'm learning to use it

Rituals for the Ruined

Back up light
One black one white
It's gonna take
An awful fight

You may see blood
You may see fire
And not the kind
That was fake with desire

Light a candle
Ten by ten
A thousand times
Surely done by then

Your step will carry
A lighter gait
Your soul rebuilt
By the hands of fate

Forever Lovers

It's painted in the stars
Inscribed upon every grain of sand
This love of ours

But the sands of time
Won't last forever
And what will be the monument
That we were ever together?

What mark will we make?
What hell on earth
Would be too much to take?

What feels like destiny
Is just a heart crying out
For a love that's true

What hurts like a God gone mad
Is but a flame of life
And it burns in you

A Christmas Alone i

I'm half drunk
And I'm sunk
Everyone I love
Is half a world away

What is this city without you?
Still so much, it's true

I have all these words
I can't bring myself to say
So I think
I'll just wash them down with a drink
At my favourite bar

I'll daydream about the things we did
And wish you weren't so far

What will it be like
When you return?
Did you warm your hands
On the fire?
Did you feel the burn
Like I did?

These questions
Have answers
Buried somewhere
Beneath the snow
Maybe by spring
We'll be a thing
But who could know?

Afterglow

Even if I cower in the corner
Like a little girl
I'll do my best
To make you feel
Like the tallest man
In the world

Even if I'm shaking
And I can't break through
I'll hurt myself
Before I ever hurt you

Because you don't know me
But you might just love me
Anyway

Maybe you can know
The person I became
Because you looked at me
That way

It's cold outside
But it's spring in my heart
Because I'm still melting
From when you opened yours

Deafening Daydreams

Where are you?
And tell me
What's on your mind?

Where are you?
Besides in my head
All the time?

What are we?
Future lovers
Or yesterday's news?

I'd listen
But I'm drowning baby
And I can't hear you

The Wasted Wallflower

What makes a wallflower
A waste of time?
You once felt a magic
That now you can't find

She's a mess
But she's magic
And she's ready for you

Under the chaos
Young blood turning blue

Wade into the water
Kill all the clocks
Immortal lake portal
Red rivers and rocks

The river that lives
Because the girl wept
Wallflower tears
She collected and kept

What makes a wallflower
A waste of time?
You've got your secrets
And God I've got mine

A Christmas Alone ii

I was wasted the first day
I was wasted so I cannot say
Where my mind was
When the morning birds
Woke you up

And I'm not thinking about
What to say
I'm laying here
Knowing we aren't the same
Knowing we can't go back
The people we once were
Out of focus, fade to black

So how can I be better like you
When wasted day one
Just ruined day two
And on day three
People expect things from me
But I'm tired

It's Christmas
And I learned something dark
It's just me here
Trying to start again
Trying to be my own friend

Licking these wounds

I gave myself

Pouring out the liquor

From the shelf

Cutting up the cigarettes

To save my health

Dreaming about who I could be

How I could see

If I could just

Open these eyes

What would it feel like

To live without lies?

Lies you told me

Lies I heard you say

To my heart

How after everything

You became my art

I needed you

To take me apart

So I could learn

To put myself together now

My Side of Your Story

I found you in the church
Where you'd been all along
Jaded with dresses
And bored of the songs

You were sweet like you meant it
And came to my door
You sat down beside me
But I wanted more

I still do
I need it
And you're taking your time
But you still call me pretty
And I try to be kind

I'm patient and gentle
Too much perhaps
We carry your baggage
And mine on our backs

1000 Rounds

I called you by your real name
And hoped it would make you smile
To hear what I had to say

Maybe it would leave me bare
Give away too much
But I couldn't think
And I couldn't care

For the first time last night
I had to have you
And feel your touch

In the midnight silhouette
The perfect man
Stood before me
It was much too much

You stand before me still
On the other side
My here and now is overflowing
With reasons why

It took 1000 rounds
Of skin on skin
To finally feel
I could let you in

Start with Scared

I got scared
When I couldn't see anymore
Then I realized
That darkness was a door

And pain was but a window
Through which I could see
All that I needed to shed
In order to be free

When one door closes
All the walls fall down
You can step outside
And take a look around

In your weakest moment
Find a strength in fear
Let it root you to the earth
Or move your legs to run from here

Folded Feelings

You told me to hold more cards
But I'm a deck away
From any

I told you I could handle it
But I'm two cents short
Of a penny

I've got nothing left to spend
Heart in half
And half again

The Last Thing You Say

What will I lose
If I let go?
I'm searching for things
I already know
Trying to keep something
I don't even own

How will it feel
To walk away?
I know
I'll be haunted forever
By the last thing you say

Ode to the Traveller

I am a traveller
A wandering soul
I wander and ponder
I scour for gold

It's not hard to find
There's magic around
In a color, a smile
In city park sounds

I don't carry maps
A compass or plans
The world spins around
In the palm of my hand

Momentos and marvels
Come home with me
Memories too
Things I treasure and keep

On buses and trains
Along for the ride
On ferries and planes
My heart opens wide

I am a traveller
Walking through life
A fiend for trouble
A sucker for strife

What fun I've had
Running it down
This dream that I'm chasing
The friends that I've found

I'll never stop leaving
I always come back
I am a traveller
I have earned that

Look Within

The gardenia gets me down
Cos I wanna walk through her
But she's not around

I gotta build my own
A place where I can be
The girl I've always known

But I searched the earth
For a plot that felt
Like what I was worth

I never knew
I couldn't see
That the only place for that garden
Was within me

Solemn Admissions

Six cigarettes
And a nightcap
On ice

I'd be lying
To say
Only thought of you
Twice

I must know
What I don't know
It's clear
Never will

But I smoke
And I drink
And I think of you
Still

Little Lighthouse

Little lighthouse
Look at at me
Show me what it is
You see

Do those ships
Just pass you by?
Did you ever
Wonder why?

Oh the seas
That brush your knees
Sailors fight
Use up your light

Little lighthouse
Come with me
Show me what it is
You see

The Psychology of Flowers

It's the point
Where you're done
When you call it
And you can't care at all

I know it will be
When the last petal falls

It will happen
When I'm gone
I won't be here anymore
To see the roses
Scattered on the living room floor

Smilodawn

The sabre tooth
Reveals the truth
A beast that morphed
To a man headed north

He's taking me with him
And taming my ways
We'll hunt through the night
And sleep through the days

No matter the danger
No matter the dark
He's an angel that howls
As the devil cries hark

And he doesn't care
That I fall and I break
He boldly goes on
With me in his wake

Over the mountains
And under the seas
The stars are the map
That sets us both free

He's taking me there
Where a cross marks the place
The centre of chaos
And order - home base

We stand in the wind
Where we'll soon part ways
The man, the tiger
The dealer of days

Don't if You Won't

Don't touch
What you can't feel
Don't break things
That you won't be able to heal

Like my heart
Don't make it beat
So god damn fast
If it's gonna stop
Every time you come close

Don't take my breath away
When I need it the most

Don't look at me baby
If you don't see
How your eyes
Devour me

Don't even think about
All of the things
You do not know

Don't lift me up
If you're just gonna
Turn around
And let me go

No Goodnight

Say something I wish you wouldn't
So I can do things I thought I couldn't
Like let you go

The best part is
Now I know
If there's no reply
You won't lie...

Asked you to be careful what you say
I know you won't anyway
I'll just watch your worthless words
Float right on by
Next time

The air is so thin up there
On your pedestal
How do your promises
Survive at all?

As you put me through hell
As I'm under your spell

Go to sleep on your own words
Wonder why I don't reply
And hurt before I hurt

The One (That Got Away)

As I ready myself
To crumble here
In the dark

I remember
It doesn't matter
Noah built an arc

For every creature
That went inside
I have a hundred heartaches
From the lovers lies

Mourning something
I never knew how to hold
Anyway

Slipped through my fingers
To be the one
That got away

The Smoky Omen

Hide the ashtray
From your mother
A storm is coming
Run for cover

Steal a second
Of your own
Fix what broke
Live all alone

Open the window
Clear out the smoke
Sit down with your soul
And build your own hope

A darkness is coming
At least this you know
It's about to get real
He's about to let you go

Pristine as the Sistine

My resting face
Looks anything but rested

There's a sadness
No smile on display
The peace that protested
And withered away

A grimace cuts in
Most of the time
A twisted grimace
Showing struggles in my mind

So take my face in your hands
And bring back the feeling
Tell me all your plans
And paint me in
Like Michelangelo
And the ceiling

The Art of Darkness

Things sound different
In the dark
Every dark thought
A work of art

Let the colors
Tell you things
As when the ocean
Swells, she sings

Comatose Crying

I want to throw up
Let the anxious feeling out
Or maybe I can yell
Let it all go in a shout

Scream it free
In an empty place
Pain pouring out
From the hole in my face

I'm too tired to smoke
If you can believe it
My third eye has to open
For the beauty; I receive it

I'll go back to sleep
For a thousand years
I won't be awake
For the coming of tears

As the feelings fall down
And slip from my eyes
Tossing and turning
Asleep through the cries

I'm trying to deal
Any way that I can
I'm half of a heart
Woman without man

Hurt Lovers Hurt Lovers

How did you bend?
Why did we break?
What make me think
That I had what it takes?

What made you shiver?
And what made us try?
What was it babe
That you saw in my eyes?

How we did get here?
And where should we go?
Now that we know
All the things that we know?

Why do we love
All the pain we inflict?
Why do we smile
When we both are just sick?

I know I am drawn
To the light in your heart
But I think that the chaos
Created every spark
That we ever felt

A Christmas Alone iii

I'm strung up you see
Like the lights on the trees
I need to let go
But I've fallen like snow

You're colder than ice rain
But the frost
Stills my tired brain

I can see my breath in the air
Like the truth:
I would know if you cared

But in the holiday cheer
I'll be without you, here

Ash in snow
Ash in snow
Thinking about
All the things you don't know

So Don't

It hurts
It'll hurt more I know
I have to look at it
Like I'll grow
But the stars have formed
In a shape just for show
Babe,
I'm gonna miss you
When you go

How to Fix a Broken Heart

But I didn't know

I have two hearts

And they're both breaking

When you're open

It's all there for the taking

People will take you

They'll break you

But darling

Let me ask you this:

If you can laugh

At your own broken heart

Are you sick

Or are you smart?

Leaving Home

Sleepy suburb
Ever holding its space
Under the Westerly

We never made each other promises
Except that you would stay
And I would leave

And I visit
Just to show you that I've changed
It's hard to see you now
Because I'm not the same

When I left you
I was but a girl
Full of dreams
Chasing the world

Now I'm a woman
Trying hard to make my mark
Now I can handle you
Because I'm jaded
In all the right parts

There's bugs
It's hot
I'm here
And they're not

I think I needed you
So I could understand
What it would feel like
To break through
And leave this town

Precursory Pain

I imagine the worst
First
So that you don't get
To take that away from me too

I close my eyes
And take a breath
What else can I do?

I never thought
That it would all come
Back around

You stand before me
And I can't look away
Somehow

Reasons for Demons

You're afraid of me
And that is ok
Most people around
Feel just the same way

They run wild from us
Because they don't understand
We exist with the good
We're the broken, the bad

It's everywhere you see
This stark duality
There are always two sides
Here's why you shouldn't hide:

We are your demons
Your worries, your fears
And we'll follow you
Haunt you
For days, weeks and years
Until you invite us
To come on inside
We'll keep chasing you
As you keep trying to hide

We want the same things
To be understood
To feel safe, to feel free
Implying hope that we could

I am your pain
Breathe in and face me
Better yet, broken one
Come out and chase me

Because once we have met
You'll understand why
It's important we listen
Try to see eye to eye

I won't go away
Until I am addressed
So take off your armor
Take back your protest

I may be a monster
But I too have a soul
And I come bearing gifts
That will lighten your load

You are afraid of me
And that is ok
But I know you are ready
Today is the day

1000 Paper Cranes

And in the new year
My living room will become
The city of 1000 cranes
Paper-made
Soldering my nerves that frayed
Hanging hope in exchange
Willowed wings
And winter days

Farthest Known Planet

Kneeling Neptune
How were you so sure?
Did you see it
In your crystal ball?

What is it
That you take me for?
I cannot love you
For I have two other
Paramours

I'm opening a golden door
I'm walking through
To leave this war

A voice told me
The best days are ahead
Forget the past
For what it gave you
Look up instead
You know
You always followed
Just exactly where
Your heart led

New Year Fear

Getting ready for another
Wild ride around the sun
Letting go of every little thing
I wished I hadn't done

And thinking about things
I should do
If I can bring myself to also
Let go of you

Petty Forever

You wrote songs
About being free
You're the reason I write
The reason I see

I saw you shine
And in your light
I discovered
Who I was supposed to be

I tell everyone
When I die, you're the one
Who's gonna come for me

Petty forever
Now my hero is free

- For Tom

My Montreal

Love the city you live in
Hug the place you call home
Leave her when you need to
She knows you need to roam

Let her take you in on days
When nothing and no one else can
Know that she has you
Know that she is you
And know
That she always has a plan

Winter Retreat

Synthetic sleep
I'm in too deep
Losing track
Of days and weeks

Time goes on
And so do we
But we aren't where
I hoped we'd be

Tired of hope
Tired of trying
The knife in the words
When you said I was lying

Cutting me up
In one thousand splinters
Breaking me down
I'll retreat for the winter

Hey Mister, That's My Big Sister

Of all the things I remember
I always admired your handwriting
The most

All the times you tricked me
And lately I remember the fighting
As if I can see our small ghosts

You traded me a dollar for two
You said it was worth more -
And I believed you

But I also believed
Things you showed me
Things you didn't need to say

In your actions
You said so much more
In an unspoken way

You taught me what it meant
To have a dream
To be determined

To never give up
To count every failure
As a necessary step
Toward any place

That would be worth it

And all these years later
I remember how
I always wanted to be you

You followed your heart
Anywhere it led
As if you could
Walk through walls
Even in years I couldn't see you

When you left home
To see the world
When I was still
A little girl

And then I left too
But it put more than the world
Between me and you

Even now we should know better
And we try to
Every second phone call
Leaves a tear on a letter

On all these letters
That I'll never send
Because I miss my sister
My best friend

So I keep them close

Because now we have

The same handwriting

And we both are sick

Of the tired fighting

And my cursive

Makes me smile

Because it reminds me of you

I know I've been gone a while

But I'll be home soon

For Kelly

Ever Clever

I'd hold a candle
To the truth
If I could find it
Where to start....

Scale the side
Of a mountain
And become
It's own art

Drink up a lake
Of loneliness
To break
Your own heart

Do what hurts
Because you should
Because you know
It's smart

Find Your Kind

Tobacco and patchouli
Because this world is too unruly
To try and do this chaos dance
Without a little ambiance

A mundane day
Is a mundane mind
So I circle the waters
In search of my kind

A little magic
And mystery too
I have found
Someone kindred in you

You give me the feeling
I had searched for so long
And could only ever find
With a drink and a song

You order the chaos
When chaos calls by
You give me a reason
To get up and try

Australia i

A month-long weekend
In a cloudless place
People that don't recognize me
Even with the same face

Roads that lead
To suburbia without trees
Memories that jarr me
I count them
I freeze

Exhale
On the ocean
And grow gentle with time
But time runs out
So I smoke and I wine

There's a reason you see
I'm learning about me
I need to let go
And speak the truth
That I know

That Song

The smoke
Of the incense
Comes at me
Aggressively

Determined as all hell
Imposing
Like it wants
To smother me

But I'm running
Out of breath
Off the land
Straight ahead
And out to sea

The Pacific Ocean
Could just swallow me
I could drown
A thousand times
And I'd still hear that song
As my lungs deplete

The Sure Earth Core

The bergamot burns
While you drift away
While the earth still turns

Here at its core
I sit still in the midst
Feeling oh so sure

That you won't be back
And honey if you're gone
I can deal with that

Cos this time
When I watched you go
It was effortless
You had to leave
So I'd know

Blue Eyes ii

I know you're down
But you wear it well
Even in the depths of hell

And I know you're scared
From putting off the fight
Hiding from nightmares

But things will turn around
You'll see
You have more than you know
And you have me

Soon you'll be free
Soon this will be
A distant memory

I promised you
So you know it's true
Trust me

-Eyes
The Bluest Blue

Your Worries < My Love

What did you expect?
That I'd say
"Get over it.
You're boring me to death
With your darkness."

You know
There's darkness in me too
And I know you better
Baby it's true

The Voice in Your Head

I know what you scream
You little voice there
Inside of me
I know exactly what you mean

But you make us both
Seem weak
You utter horrors
I'd be ashamed to speak

If I were stronger
There would be no you
Little voice there
I'd be unconsumed

Nothing in my ear
Breathing in the untrue
Breathing out fear
Choking black and blue

And to you I say, hey
Maybe it goes both ways
It's exactly the same
But who would wanna
Play those games

Little voice there
Why do I even care?

A Rhyme of Time

Time is the painful
Axe that grinds
Striking a blow
Cutting straight through the spine

Taking away
What we thought we had left
Teaching us emptiness
Evil, and theft

Time doesn't care
If you're coming or going
It's the stubbornest thing
She's cruel and she knows it

No one can stop her
She's vast and she's deep
She's made up of minutes
You know you can't keep

We watch her go by
Only too late to see
The moment has passed
Oh, what could have been

Untethered Feathers

I found a fractal
In the frozen ground
A shard from your heart
A note from its sound

A bleeding slither
At first I was still
Then I began to quiver
The flower in your heart
Had begun to wither

So I cried across time
Back to when your spirit
Was entwined with mine
Under a star spun sky
I prayed to the great pines

We lost touch
So you sparked a fire
Now all these years have passed
And we are walking wires

Attached to nothing at all
I swear one missed breath
I would slip and fall
No one would hear my call...

Deep and Shallow

It's going to keep
But how would we ever know?
And I stand here looking deep
Catching flakes of snow
So I can show

All the colors that I held inside
Because I try to run
And I always hide

I need to know where they are
So I can plot the city like the stars
Map them and navigate these scars
Even if I can, I can't

This One's For You

I hope you're enjoying the weather
While I sit here
Trying to keep it together

I hope you wake up each day
Smiling
Ready to face
Whatever comes your way

While I wrestle with what to say
Every time I open my mouth
And go to speak
Praying that nobody knows
That I'm scared
And I'm weak

Remembering
That everybody feels like this
Sometimes
Everybody goes through the hell
That I mistake
As only mine

And the strangest thing of all
Is I address you
Like I know you
Like I know who to call

I have no idea who you are
But I know that you're better
You shine the brightest
You are the North Star

Important Questions

Have you ever travelled
To places that weren't real?
Have you ever touched someone
You couldn't feel?

Have you ever told a lie
That you believed was true?
A lie you lived alongside
While it cut and burned you?

Did you wake up to find
That nothing was the same?
A face in the mirror
A body with no name

But the scene has changed
An ocean of regret
The vastness overcame

Would you dive right in
And never take the blame?
Would you let that current take you
Pounded, sorry
Wave by wave?

You can't take back
All that you gave
But you can take this hand
And become a man saved

Answers in Eden

Things that I'm afraid to admit
Places where I feel I don't fit
They grow by the day
Never sure what to say
What happened to my courage
Lord, this can't be it

Bring me solace
And a gentle hand
Let me walk with ease
And speak the truth on command
Give me strength
To find a kind of peace
I once had

This is a prayer
A fable told to me
By a man who cared
A poem filled with riddles
That he kindly shared
I'm picking up the pieces
Scattered everywhere
Spread beneath the palms of Eden
If I ever get there

Crushed

My heart was an open field
You ran through it
Set fire to it

But when the sun went down
You said in cold blood
You didn't do it

The Daily Do Over

The greatest thing to discover
Is that you think you know yourself
But you actually don't
And that you can do everything
You think you won't

That you can trust yourself
And grow your own hope
That the best it yet to come
After the coming undone
And the do over you get
Each day

That you don't hold all the answers
And that is ok
"Beware of unearned wisdom"
I heard a wise man once say

That your armor isn't made of steel
But of vulnerability
And your greatest weapon
Is a sensibility

You know it, my dear
You're in a thing
A phase that will pass
It's for wisdom you earned
This aching won't last

Breathe in, breathe out

Steady your hand

I take it in mine

It's me you understand

Welcome Wings

Won't you give me something sweet
To soothe my sorry soul
I'm feeling incomplete

Won't you send me a postcard
From your side of town
So I can remember what it felt like
To have you around

I've been keeping my ear to the ground
Not to keep up with the times
But because I fell down
Sometimes cliches come in rounds

One day you'll call me out
On asking for so much
Because you won't have anything
Left to give
Except your word, your touch

And I'll tell you that I'm sorry
For the awful things
You'll tell me not to worry
Words are welcome wings

Where the Wonderful Things Go

It's the smoke
That you don't exhale
It's the place
Where the colour
In your face goes
When you're turning pale

It's the man you know
That you don't recognize
Anymore
And the room with only windows
When you need a door

And your heart hits the floor
The pit of your stomach
It hurts to be so sure

It's the truth
That falls right out of your lies
And the smile that disappears
In the choke of your cries

It's the youth
When you're growing old
And the warmth you miss
When it's grey and it's cold

It's the story they told
Of the man on horseback
In the desert
Who found blood, not gold

One for One

A penny for your problems
To distract me from mine
A dollar for your daydreams
And a wish for your wine

We will make an exchange
An offering true
I'll give you my garden
If you give me yours too

Tailored Temptress

I'm a lady of lace
And a woman of extremes
I'm nice in your nightmares
But dark in your dreams

Out of focus
And running
Playful but sure
And you follow me down
But you're caught
You've been lured

Be Careful What You Kiss For

I wanted to be
Like the girls that you admired
I wanted that flame
But all flames come from fire

Fire that burns
Through the soles of our feet
I'd dance with the devil
If he said something sweet

Omma Moon

I never did look at it
When I was up close
It's like we don't see
The things we need the most

Sometimes from afar
But I'd forget when I got nearer
The moon in the window
It couldn't be clearer

The heavens inside
In the room
In us all
The cosmos beckons
Answer the call

Remnants

Fill up
What I believed to be empty
All this time

Take away everything
That I understood
To be mine

One day
There will be nothing left
But the memory of me
Will remember you

The painful truth
Of existence
Cuts deep

I want you so much
But you're not a thing
I can keep

You're a man
And we live in moments
Through time

Time is made up of days...

One day
There will be nothing left
But the memory of me
Will remember you

The Southern Sorry Sea

An apology
Painted so vividly
And erased in a gesture
That had no reply

Because I'd rather extend
This olive branch
Than an artfully twisted lie

I didn't realize
It would only hurt us both
You were just trying to get by
Just trying to cope

There was an ocean between us
Wet with my wrongs
Waves of regret
I had poured into songs

I flooded the fairytale
Corrupted the files
Burned down the village
All with a smile

According to you
But the smile was fake
Cos our love had grown wings
Just to drown in a lake

I always remember
The sick disbelief
How could the right thing
Cause us such grief?

So I'm sorry
I call back, to the people
We were before
A message through time
But it doesn't matter anymore

The damage is done
Fate has now won
An apology, an analogy
The story she spun

How I'll Know

Like the forbidden fruit
You opened my eyes
I wasn't supposed to touch you
It wasn't wise

But you penetrate my soul
Until the only thing I know
To be true
Is the way to go:
Towards you

Ever closer
Crossing deserts
And the tundra, oceans, skies and plains
Through battering winds
And pouring rains

I'll come to you
We'll meet there
But if you don't show
I'll bow my head
And let you go

The Girl and the Tea

It took her forever
But she made it with love
On the hand that poured milk
Was a soft velvet glove

I guess she didn't see
Any reason to hurry
It must be so nice
Just to live without worry

She twirled to reach cups
Pull steam knobs and whistles
Her dress was of flowers and roses
Not thistles

She was going to Ireland
But my tea was from London
And the cups had cute little
Stamps printed on them

I wanted to tell her
She brightened my day
Brought a smile to my face
In her own little way

I'll be back another day
To get me some more
But for now, my sweet tea
I'm tired and sore

Disintegrate

Sad eyes
Crying like a phoenix
And she cries
Curled up in the shell
Not strong like Venus

To come to me
In a dream
Means I need to be asleep
That's what it means

But I've spent so long
So tired
An eternal sleep must end
It's time

I hear violins
And I want to spread my wings
I'm opening up
And I'm everything

Red Wine, White Out

Crimson and Cream
I can't see through
And the colours are mean

I'll steep myself
In your tea
So sugar sweet
You'll dream of me

You'll turn around
And see yourself
In all my songs

And I'll have given away
What I failed so good
To hide all along

Red wine
White out
Can't scream
Can't shout

Love v Pain

If we love love
Why don't we hurt pain?
If we taught it a thing or two
Couldn't we stop it
From hurting us again?

But we're addicted
To the feeling we get
Even still
When todays chances
Become tomorrow's regrets

And our love lines tell a story
The shape of its colour
Keeps the secrets safe

The things we never learn
That we forget
When it becomes
Another one
We're dreaming of

A Ravaging

Fill me up
With what I require
Drown me in darkness
Then set me on fire

Bury me deep
In a sea of regret
Fanning the flames
Climbing still higher yet

The Artful Goodnight

Paint me with the brush of sleep

Colour me slumbered

Awake is a palette I do not

Want to keep

Right now

Or use

And let me go gently

For the fools we are

Haunt me

And we're fools

Aplenty

Such heathen hues

Nicotine Fables

Count them all
Every cigarette butt
You ever tossed away

That's how many thoughts
That I have of you each day

But I don't burn them up
I hold them dear
And they get me by
Until next you are near

Hotel Hopeless

He lopes through the lobby
Looking around
Nursing a cup
Of that Old Fashioned sound

Comfortable, curious
He fits in this world
In the darkest blue velvet
Before ten thousand girls

But he'd never know it
The feeling he causes
A heart's endless video
That plays without pauses

Hell is the people
That are not him
But unless I let go
I'll be stuck in this sin

Stuck watching the scene
Play again and again
Dying inside while he
Moves on and then

Where will I be
When he's old and he's married?
Will my heart survive
Seeing my love as it's carried?

Away in a suitcase
That someone else owns
How cruel is this picture
This dish of unknowns

That I'm forced to dine on
Night after night
Is life now just me trying
To survive one long fight?

I fight it and fight it
But I cannot let go
And that man in the lobby
I swear that he knows

That makes it harder
To pretend that I'm fine
Maybe one day
I'll believe my own rhyme

I'll fall for the riddle
I write late at night
And I'll see him beside her
Maybe it will feel alright

Left on Love

You wanted me to be good
But I was to good
As darkness is to light
Evil and evasive
Faking wrongs for right

You wanted more
Than I could ever give you
You wanted to be sure
That I would never leave you
But to be fair
Love left me too...

And look at what she made me do
When she came back in spades
She held me out over the ledge
And drew back the shades

For all the world to see what I had done

"Need Pain for Art"

Sometimes I think
You were just a distraction
Something nice to look at
While my world was falling apart

And other times
I think
You were the catalyst
That broke the ground
Beneath my art

A Kingdom Cursed

The funeral of the Irish Queen
We do not know of things
We have not seen

So she goes before us
And we sing the days away
Regretting every chorus

Because we should never
Have let her go
Our Queen had fallen
And all the land
Took a mighty blow

They didn't know
The worst was yet to come
Things seem so together
Until they come undone

Dearest Depthless

You taught me how to let go
But now I never want to
Let go of you

I see in your reflection
The deepest expanse
That a human could be

I recognize
I'll never really know you
But I promise I'll try

Monarchs in March

What is a butterfly without wings?
And who is a bird that doesn't sing?
I'm a soul filled with love
I have never been without it

I am a singing butterfly
Love tells me all about it

On a breeze that carries truth
I find my spirit there
It brings me peace
Clarity and hope
It's the blue in your sultry stare

It's when I'm underneath
When I'm crawling up the slope
It's home, a place I come back to
To find myself

It's every book I ever read
And placed back on the shelf

It captures me
And takes me in every time
It's the justice that beckons
The partner in all my crimes

It's true love

Me and this life of lust

And every time I lose my way

In this I can trust

I am a singing butterfly

Now you understand why

The Sun Sayer

Copernicus
Was better than us
His seeded soul
Was spun from gold

Thistles borne
Upon his neck
Thrones built with stones
From a place called
HECK

He didn't care
For a cross to bare
Your sins were yours
And you could have more

He'd watch
And wait
Take the hint
Take the bait

Gather round
You all hearty
This is all part
Just part of the party

South Porcupine Fine

If these walls could walk
They'd stay right here
Holding the home they bore
Year after year

Winters on winters
Northernmost land
The place it all started
Born with sticks
In their hands

Blades on their feet
Blue eyed brunettes
With cherub-kissed cheeks
Grace you'd never forget

Yours is a story
A tale from Timmins
The gold miners worshipped
The game
And their women

And o by the tower
The airport
The forest
You can taste the fir trees
If you notice the North breeze

It's a moment
A place
A memory
Enlaced

The baby blues
Stare back at you
Now from a man's face

A man
Most sincere
Who returns
Every year

No stretch to mention
His father built town
He built every inch
His son wears my crown

If these walls could walk
O they wouldn't go far
Perhaps just to see
Through the snow
To the stars

For the MacQuarries

Merciful Music

The day you hear your first song
The one that you wrote
You'll never get that day twice

And that day
My darling darkness
Is the very first day
Of the rest of your life

You know
This is how
You will learn to let go

Letters You Won't Send

A tear, and a toothache
Two years past our due date
For parting, we broke
Not a memory was spoke

Our bond obliterated
How we cried of the fated
How could I let go?
How could you not have known?

You gave me a world
In exchange for your girl
I would never be more
Had to leave to make sure

Now I chase down the demons
And they haunt me each season
To have left - to have stayed
It was not just a game

I learned on this land
I was burned by my own hand
And my flame, as it were
Not contained - you were burned

I can say, I can wish
That you'll understand this
I was wrong in my way
I would redo that day

If the sands of time could defy

Gravity, so would I

I'd do you no wrong

Like I said, vowed in song

But now and here

I cry this one tear

My tooth is still aching

And my heart

Endlessly breaking

Uncertainty

Uncertainty
Don't call here
Anymore

Forget my face
Forget my number
Forget I existed at all

There has to be a way
For me to be my own saviour
To make it through just one day

Uncertainty
Angels beckons me
While devils threaten me
Someone tell me
How to breathe

Because I feel like it's coming
Maybe I deserve it
I've spent two years running

It's like the darkness
Bares a pattern
That I never noticed

I just thought
That the light

Intermittently
Lost its focus

But I was so blind
I hid things
I thought you would never find

Because it worked in the past
But those demons can run
And they run fucking fast

They hide in the shadows
Live under rocks
And watch you
From behind trees
Biding time, taking stock

They thrive on your weakness
They know it by name
Uncertainty
Perfectly
To them it's all just a game

Walking Through Winter

It's not even snow
It's more like glitter
And I'm walking through it
In awe
It's reminding me
Not to be bitter

Not to drink that drink
With every thought
Comes bitterness
So it's better not to think

Not to drown in this
Whatever wonderful, woeful
Lesson it is

To the people who left
Their Christmas lights on
After the holidays
Bless you
In one thousand ways

Maybe this can be
My new normal
Tea for tea

Some suffering for supper
Me out walking with me

I saw a girl grinning

Running towards her love

And I saw

Three whole people

Go in for a hug

And we didn't know it

But you were giving me a gift

Not the son of God

That gave me this

Dreamscape at the Pearly Gates

Hold on to hope
To ride through your wars
Hold on to heaven
You'll get, you'll get yours

Nothing is nowhere
And no one can heed
The heart that you carry
The blood that you'd bleed

Boredom, she beckons
The sacred come second
The wisdom in words
Flown by air, borne by birds

Now silence in silver
Who darns in her sleep
Strings made so tidy
Tarnished, torn just to keep

O lightning struck gold
Nought for treasure
Cotton cold

Shouldered by demons
That would gild every season
Stolen for harmless
And forgotten reasons

Sick Saint Nick

There's nothing like
A hotel lobby at Christmas
I can appreciate the beauty of it
But I can't afford to see a dentist

We either move along
In masquerade
Or drink about
How we all got played

Singing carols
While the new year hides
Around the bend
Watching us break
Merry madness
More than any man
Could take

Tie a ribbon around
All that you wish to forget
That's your Christmas wish
But it's no more
Than a Yuletide bet

Messages From Moons Far Away

I think this soul
Is ready for the sun
It's dramatic
But these bones are colder
Than anyone's

I forget that I'm free
I'm not yet thirty three
Like you were
Last year

I don't know where I am
Just that I got myself
All the way here

And I forget
That this was my dream
A wakeful dream
An intention
Stronger than steel
Oh and louder than screams

I was all mixed up
Crying hopelessly
In the summer sun
And then I laughed
At the frozen moon
As it whispered to me:
"What's done is done"

Perfect Penance

Sure
I can bite my tongue tonight
I've done it before

But why does tonight
Hurt like no other night?
Like a new kind of war

Why does every song
Scream to me secrets
While I drink wine for dinner
In the dark
On the floor?

As I try to drown out
What I thought I heard
"This is your perfect penance
You are paying only
For what you deserve."

Send Yourself to Me, When You Discover Who You Are

When everything hurts
And nothing's ok
When it takes half a heart
Just to get through the day

When silence is painful
And louder than jets
You are the murmur
The deeper it gets

The Gift

If I had been your first choice
I never would have found my voice
The cried crescendo that ensued
The pining, pain and platitudes

If I had had you, fair and square
With no other to compare
I wouldn't know
I'd never see
The devil that had drowned in me

I danced with him
An evil fugue
He tricked me into
Wanting you

He took my hands
And made them quiver
I'd shake the shake
I'd shake and shiver

Full of worry
Sick with doubt
I longed for all I dreamt about

Lost for words
And muted more
I wondered what I'd waited for

So in the songs I sailed away
The music made me
Act this way

No sooner than a fallen tear
It had somehow been a year
And there you were
With words and whispers
As if time had stopped
As if nothing had shifted

But it would be remiss of me
To have somehow failed to see
The year that was
One long, cold night
Was poetry I could rewrite

Vandalized Vessels

I couldn't hear the answers
From deep down in the depths
Of your cavernous heart

But I could hear my own whispers
As I felt my way through
The grateful dark

And in the shadows
There were remnants
Of some ravenous art

As if even in your thoughts
And prayers
I was being
Torn apart

Moon Raking Faker

The Sailor swore
That he would stay
But sailors do that
So they say

In sleight of hand
Much more than most
He tore up hearts
From coast to coast

Last I heard
He found the one
A likely story
A setting sun

In all the stars
On all the seas
That sailor never
Heard my pleas

To dock the ship
To set her free
But he waved
As waves unravelled me

I'd been tossed over
The sailors boat
My heart was too heavy
To keep me afloat

And so once more
In the very next town
While the sailor was swearing
I cried as I drowned

Now there's a ghost
At the depths of the sea
The man with the mouth
Was the ending of me

Time Heals All Fools

The sight of me
Cools your shoulder
Like you wouldn't believe

Unexpected
After all this time
More than I could have dreamt
All the days that I have pined

Although you visited me
In those nightmare visions
Clear as day
For the daylight giveth

And my eyes runneth over
Crying wine that I cannot touch
And your words were never softer
More sincere
It meant so much

But the whole galaxy of us
Sits on a tiny shelf
Where the mile ends
And every star-crossed memory
Of us blinking, fading
As my patience bends

How did you let go
Yet hold on
At the same time
To us, to me?
What you remember
Is clouded with lies
About who you wanted
Us to be

But this is the most
Fitting end
Where an end had already
Come before

One day you'll smile
As I pass by
And you'll mean it
Finding flowers at your door

Notes From Places I Shouldn't Have Been

Treading water
Spinning gold
I am turning
Tales untold

As I sip
The sea
She shrinks
She offered me
A thousand drinks

So I took them all
Come hell and she would
As the waves died down
I soon understood

The serpent will test you
Mirages not real
The mother will bless you
Don't fight how you feel

Play Pretend, Your Heart Will Mend

Baby is your pain
This romantic?
I saw them together
They were dancing

Once I let it floor me
No guilt, no shame
If you leave me behind
It's just not the same

Your silence
Is the loudest message
I could ever receive

Even though you speak
In the long lost language
Of make believe

Fire Sale: Things I'll Trade For Love

The truth is in the part
Where you stole and broke my heart
The story started long before
The man that I want more and more

A glimpse of love
A touch so soft
I'd give up everything I lost

I'd hand it over
Piece by piece
For the longest, slowest,
Most painful release

Do I deserve this?
I don't know
But I shake
And I shake
I refuse to let go

Do I love you more
Than I love myself?
I wrote the book
And you built the shelf

You made me whole
This broken, lost soul
Through the coldest of winters
Through the shudders
The shivers

Foresight the Flashlight

They were dancing
Kissing
Talking close
And I thought it was real

I realized then
I should have thought about
How this would feel

What do you do
When you find
Everyone you ever loved
Left you behind

At least when you're alone
No one hears your cries
You're a tree falling in the forest
You are free falling
Let's be honest

Little Prayers for All Your Cares

I'd rather have a soft soul
Than a cigarette
I'd rather turn wine into water
So that I could forget
All the chances I didn't take
Baby I will bend
So that you don't break

Her First Show

Reading the room
As if people were pages
Like lines from a sonnet
A song for the ages

And if you do utter
In words to this crowd
Make sure you mean them
Say them out loud

Tell them your secrets
Or tell them your lies
But they came here to listen
So think and be wise

Sing what you feel
And give them that shiver
The room is a garden
With snakes that do slither

This is your show
The one that you wanted
Howl like a hunter
The ghost that you haunted

And then take a bow
Thank them with grace
As they simmer the spotlight
In golden good taste

Reading the room
As if people were pages
Like lines from a sonnet
A song for the ages

For Lisa

A Poem on Poems

Things don't make sense
If they don't rhyme
So I speak in song
To pass the time

I have to think in poetry
Each one is a letter
From me to me

I write and I write
They never stop coming
To keep it inside
Would be cold and mind-numbing

I laze over lyrics
And they help me to see
Each one is a letter
From me, to me

The Glow You Know

I heard somebody light up
And I turned away
Can't set this soul on fire today

Can't tell me that I won't get burned
In a world where sparks
Are spent unearned

Unworthy in their lust for light
Unwilling players in the fight
Yearning just to get it right
Wonders never were so white

Over (and Out)

The broken circle on my hand
The nights we spent
The days in sand

The hourglass is now complete
The letting go that feels so sweet

Surprised to find
Something left
The pull
The residual

It takes two to make a mess
Like we did
Like we always did

It was our mess
But I must admit
It's over baby
This is it

You can blame me
All you like
You can hate me
For every fight
But you felt it too
So wrong
So right

It was never meant to last
A story we tell
From the past

You'll never understand
How much you gave me
In the end
It was the pain that saved me

I'm not afraid of anything now
Even letting go

Crying Thunder

It smells like rain
And I think to myself
I don't wanna do this again

I don't wanna cry
While it pours outside
I don't want grey
To be the color of this day

I want clear skies
But they open up
And the thunder cries...

On Hope

Every day is an ordeal
Every day I learn
That a thing I feared
Has become real
Hell is when frustration
Can no longer be concealed
But if we can spin ourselves
Into darkness
Can we also make believe
That we are healed?

The Like-Minded Lost

I forgot to tell you
I've never seen the sun
I've danced around the truth
In the dark
But I can't be the only one

Beware of the Bright and Beautiful

You came from a volcano
Bound north
Because you heard it was
The way to go

You keep your precious things
In places no one else
Dares to visit

It's not for your beauty
That they stay away
Or is it?

I fell asleep listening
To a story about butterflies
A story of fascination
And wonder
As I closed my eyes

I Loved You at the Lake

I wanted to tell you
When we were by the lake's edge
But I held my tongue

Then on Broadway and Main
It came over me again
But the words were unsung

If there's one thing I've learned
With you
I can take my time
And that's just how you like it

With a flower in my hair baby
One of these days
I won't have it in me to fight it
Anymore

Walking through your sleepy town
Discovering another piece of you
Breaking new ground

This is where you got
Your golden heart
And I'm mining it for reasons
We should ever be apart

Lacrimation

Tears don't leave a stain
Not like blood
Not like blood, baby
But it's a different pain

Do red eyes see the rain
Differently?
Do you cry because you're strong
Or because you're weak?

After the flood
That comes down your cheeks
Will the drought bring
The answers you seek?

Coastlines

I walked the coastlines of this life
Picking up shells
Of what was left behind

Though beautiful
Each one left me more confused
Trying to follow the stars
That led me back to you

I follow coastlines
Because the land tells lies
I walk on water
Because I heard it's wise

We know that the moon
He pulls the tide
When the sun isn't looking
It's so easy to hide

We know that the sky
Has a story to tell
The astrologers whispered
We were under their spell

I follow coastlines
Because the land tells lies
I walk on water
Because I heard it's wise

Enshrined

Oh the beauty
Of watching your walls
Come down

In the vapour
Of your whisper
I swear I could drown

And I don't have to
Keep up with you
But I want to

Moments on Corners

We were throwing our cigarettes
Down the drain
While we talked of troubles
In the soft summer rain

You were thinking
Of how well this all played out
I was thinking
I'll adore you
Until my lungs give out

We're two wings
On the same bird
To lift each other up
And run away from the herd

When we can't find the words
But there's so much to say
We don't even need to talk
When you look at me that way

Missing: Faith, and the Way

Bring me a butterfly
And a broken dream
Because I've lost my way

Let her wings be the colour
Of the sun in the sky
On a cloudless day

Bring me hope and good cheer
Because I'm in a heap
And I've had a year

Let me find the faith I need
To not turn and run
But to stay right here

Mexico, Mi Amor

Airfields and corn fields
Below as you sleep
Patchworks of green
That I want us to keep

In just a few hours
We'll be far away
In the last 24
I gave you some greys

Misadventures we meet
As we try to survive
Teach me to breathe
While you walk by my side

Airfields and corn fields
In such long gone snow
We're a bird in the sky
Down to sweet Mexico

Remember the beach
Made our eyes so blue
Don't forget the week
When I fell in love with you

Souls Without Borders

You think you understand yourself
But you're endless
You'll never find the answer
No matter how hard you try
The day you let go
In the day you finally know
Man never did find
Where the universe ends
It's up to you to learn
How far your own borders
Can extend

The Devil Downstairs

Did you invite
The devil to dinner?
The devil downstairs
The one they call a sinner

Did you sit right down to dine
Only to see
Only to find

The devil downstairs
Doesn't eat
When he wines

He drinks the cold blood
From your broken heart
And for dessert
He'll take you right apart

Made of Mistakes

When you get your own vision
When you get it
What it is and what it isn't

But the dizzying lows
Let down like no one knows
High on the regret
Of everything you can't forget

Trading in the workhorse
For the best bet racer
And you're focused
Like a laser
On the wrong things

And the sorry singer sings
A lullaby
Woven wings
When you're only made of wool
It's hard to fly

Mirages

I only miss the idea of you
Because looking back
Isn't looking through
Memory paints over facts
With fiction
Loving you
Was a lonely affliction

Tigers in Treetops

A sound came into earshot
And it was something familiar
Something that my soul forgot

A feeling I had left behind
As I left my body
And lost my mind

I flew away
I understood things
Nobody could say

I found a new land
Where all that grew was green
And all the seas had sand

A broken window
And a crowded room
Brought me back to earth
A silver second too soon

And in treetops
Tigers slept
Under the blue moon
While a sound came into earshot...

High as Birds

I've seen the monster
I can be
When I don't try

And I've caught
Flightless birds
By their wing-tipped words
Just to get high

And I followed you
Not knowing why
Or what else to do

I followed you
Just to get high
In hope that I might
Find the truth

If I were Music

I wanna feel
As good as you look
Right now

I'm like a song
Without a hook
A mystic melody
That is incomplete
A chorus composure
Without a verse
Without a beat

And no simple key change
Will fix what's been said aloud
No words written
Nor harmonized
Could clear away the clouds
That have gathered
Across the sky of my eyes

Everlasting

Come to me stranger
Know not my name or my face
Take my hand
Mystery man
And run us out of this place

Show me moments
Where there's no divide
Between good and evil
Space inside

A place that's pure
Show me how to be sure
Or not, and to not care either way

Show me there's such a thing
As an everlasting day

Messages from the Right Ventricle

I go there sometimes
When you're not there too
I wake up in the night
Thinking of you

I long and I pine
Thinking of things that are mine
That are not you
And I think of all the things
That we could do

Of the things we could be
If we were 'us'
Wondering if we could
Pull out some kind of love
From this lust

Cos it feels nice
Sometimes it even feels right
I thought there was nothing
That could ever make me
Not wanna fight
For you

It's the voice of my whole heart
Telling me what to do

The sound of my own song

Singing to the tune

Of what we've known all along

It isn't right

It never was...

Still Present

Something starts
When everything stops
When you still your heart
You begin to get lost

In darkness
In silence
Breathe in
Breathe out

In that moment
Pure kindness
You begin to lose count

Of seconds and minutes
Time doesn't exist
The stillness speaks volumes
I can promise you this

Watch where you're going
Be where you are
Stand up for something
And you will go far

Wherever you are
There you should be
I am the moment
Ever met me?

Denial, Determination, Acceptance and Friends

I like serenity
Taking the fall
And making a mess
Out of you and me

I walk everywhere
Taking it in
Finding things
Other people don't see

I love you
Like I hate
The last drag
Of my cigarette:
Not at all

But I'll climb over
Everything you put
In front of me
The wallflower
Becomes the wall

I won't panic
Like before
When you call it all off
Because I know
Just what it takes

And I've invested
Every part of me
In this romance
That became a race

We can't compare
Don't look for me in her
Because I'm not there
And I don't care

I'm marrying the music
Because she sings to me
Whether you love me or not

And she'll give me everything
And more
That I showed you I needed
And never got
Here's to the magic
We cross oceans to find
I hope you find yours
Cos baby
You're not mine

Measured

You were always gonna
Leave me behind
It should have been clear

I'm starting to hate you

But if I'm gonna hate you
As much as I loved you
We're in trouble my dear

Poise x Arrows

Grace
Come back calling
Poise and arrows
Showing me the way

I've faced
The fallen
And I've tasted
A new day

She breezes past
And they wonder
"What has she done?"

But they don't know
She's dying inside
Because she's not
The only one

Soon enough
It's been too long
And I start to shake

Soon enough
It's coming undone
Beginning to break

Grace
Come back calling
Poise and arrows
Showing me the way

Evidence of Elements

Music and muses
It's the apple of her eye
She chooses wit over worry
And takes a slice of lies

This time it's hot
This time it's fire
It's a stroll in the park
But she's walking a wire

And it's overdue
A wave of emotion
The sky looked down
And kissed the ocean

Cordis Abyss

They tell me it's muscle memory
But my heart is a muscle
And all it remembers
Is how to beat for you

How to pound
How to ache for you
Anytime you're near
How to swell and burst
And break in half

It takes me
And it happens so fast...

Disconnected Affection

Take the heat
Off our terrible tune
Cos the world doesn't stop
While we're licking our wounds

We trace the harsh lines
Of things we must do
I remember the nights
Feeling far, close to you

As fall takes its hold
And the leaves pile low
I circle the earth
And return to the snow

Longer than Roses

Maybe I'll decide to be fine
Maybe it's ok
That you'll never be mine

The roses you gave me
Are wilting and dying
I'd give them some water
But I'm so tired of crying

Buried in books
I'll swim through the winter
I'll survive this
And what's more
I know that I need it

I need this pain
In order to grow
It's something I just
Instinctively know

I'm starting to think
I'm on the brink
Of something real

I'll let every part
Of my body
Just feel

Ville Marie

The cigarettes are cheaper
On this side of town
The place where I'd live
If I was around

And the sea breeze is sweet
But I need Ville Marie
The mountain is sweeter
She understands me

I belong near that street
Right there on the main
There is the river
She seals up my veins

What is to be
Of the ones I leave here?
Worry won't help them
And neither will fear

I will leave
It's the only answer I find
We cannot go back
We cannot rewind

Here they don't understand
But there are those that do
Far, far away
I'm coming for you

I'm down to the week
That I leave this place
On the morning flight
They'll remember my face

And the songs that I sung
When they gave me the chance
Everyone heard them
And I looked at the plants

I saw the horizon
I stared her right down
If I went in too deep
I might have just drowned

So I pack and I pine
For that place far away
For the friends and the foes
That bring light to my day

Even the demons
Fit me better out there
I won't look back
I'll try not to care

When they said goodbye
My family, old town
I said I'd stop smoking
If they burned this place down

Message in a Bottle

I talked to you
In a conversation alone
In an irony coloured coral
On my own

It felt like a cold dark room
When I needed an open field
A world away
You held your silence
You wouldn't yield

You were dirty and dark
We ran through the fire escape
And you became my art

And when the cell tower fell down
I sent a message in a bottle
So you could hear my sound

The sound of me walking free
As an empty bottle sailed the seas

Gin and Clouds

You ask me what's going on
What's going off?
Drink for a year, I say
And then stop

Just to see where you are
And realized the path you took
Took you long and far
In the wrong direction
In your introspection

Wrong to whom?
You can't smile in this darkened room
But you followed the stars
All the way to the moon
Darling, don't you see?
You aren't fooling me

Lightning in Slow Motion

He get this look in his eyes
An audacity I've seen before
He knows what he wants
And will say anything to get it

Is this what you want?
Or is this what you want
Right now?

Am I it?
Am I the one
You want to keep around?

And it keeps me guessing
They say we like that
But it's hard and messy

Keeping up with you
Is like lightning in slow motion
In a crowded room

You want to move
But the light is burning up the darkness
And you smell the fumes

But it's beauty
Because there are others there
Who can go down too

Only they're all you
In another dress
Each one knows he's the devil
But they all say yes

He might not know it
But he has power
Of an unholy kind
One touch can tell you
Stories of a thousand lives

You can't let go
Forever holding on
To what feels like the only thing
You will ever truly know

You're in the grips
Of the deepest kind of love there is
Your heart is just an organ
But now your soul is his

Faceless Beasts and Graceless Feats

I am the beast
Beneath my own skin
I have you in sight
And so now I begin

The journey will hurt
In the best kind of way
The pain will remind me
That I've won one more day

That with each one
The past is yet further
And with each one more
I'll be richer with fervor

Stronger and calmer
Proud and with grace
A grace that I lost
When I forgot my own face

To Be an Artist

I work in extremes
As I live out my dreams
Carving up chaos
All is not as it seems

I'm taking my time
Spilling water and wine
Losing all hope
Losing my mind

That's what it takes
To create works of art
You make yourself sick
And you break your own heart

Just to capture the essence
Of something unique
That for thousands of years
All our children will speak

Of the greatness
That came from madness
A man cut off his ear
Just to feel the sweet pain
Just to taste the sweet fear

So I work in extremes
Because I can't feel anything
In the in-betweens

I dance on the border

Between chaos and order

Because boring is no fun, dear

All is not as it seems

The Girl in the Mirror

You can write it off
As a false start
What's a week to you
In a total of fifty two
Be kind baby
Have a heart

Take it easy on yourself
Don't let the demons
Take everything
When you're stuck frozen
And nothing makes sense
You can still sing

Sing
Even if the tears come down
Sing to an empty room
Say a silent prayer
And then take a bow

Because you have
More than you know
All the things you own
Aren't always out on show

You have spirit
People who love you
And you have me

I live on the other side
Of the mirror
We have always been friends
You just don't always see

I know that it's hard
I know that it's been two years
And I know right now
You are facing your darkest fears

But tomorrow is another day
Another miracle
After sleep, awaits

Our tomorrow is a thing
Of God's grace
And if we want
We can make it painless
Coloured, fearless
Everything in its place

The Implicated and the Underwhelmed

Layers fall away
Revealing only truth
The thing you're supposed
To stand and shout
The thing that tarnished
All of you

A word said aloud
Can be taken back
But an action is forever
Can you handle that?

You didn't deserve the bad
Now I don't deserve any good
You say
That people will understand
But baby they never could

And you blew it all away
While demons laughed
In your face
You're out there in the world
But it's a lonely place

You can give your body away
A million times over
But it will never
Get you back your heart

Here you are pretending
It's a work of art

To stare down
The roman god
Is to feel your heart break
While he simply nods

Buried Treasure

In the darkest of days
I was my own
Bright light
Shining, oh so clear
It was a fight
The good fight

I built myself
A set of armor
I made the strongest shield
For the hardest nights

But in a second
It could all burn down
Your lungs are heaving
With the loudest sound
Your voice is shaking
We are coming down

The best part about
Your lowest lows
Is that the only way
Left to go
Is up
The only thing that's right
Is the light
The way that it glows

Your voice is shaking

We are coming down

But this time

I'm not dreaming

I found you in the fight

It was you that I found

The Honest Lie

I am an honest woman
Standing before you
Without broken-hearted shame
Admitting that I lost the game
But here before you
All the same

I've stared in the faces
Of the women
Who took my places
And the women
Whose places I hold

It's not creeping
If you're crying
And it's Christmas
And you're alone
And cold

It's true
I'd rather tell the truth
I'd rather pay that cost
Than pretend
To have moved on
And let go of what I lost

No
I will carry that forever

It's written on the stars
In my eyes
These eyes
That other women look at
With their own
Haven't we all lied?

I am an honest woman
On my knees before you
Down here just trying
To find the truth

Because on the ground
I hear the hopefull sound
As it speaks
To me and you

Haunted by the Hopeful

Waiting on a whisper
I waited all this time
Knowing that you kissed her
As the blood raced to my spine

Ready for the feeling
That would strike me
In good time

Leaving with a locket
And a love
That was not mine

My eyes peel
These city streets
For you
After all this time, still
Against my will

Kin in Sin

We're not that different
You and I
We both get lost
From time to time

We sharpen our arrows
And ready our bows
Shooting at stars
So they'll have the same scars

I thought I saw you
I thought I saw you
And it cut me in two

I thought I heard you say
You swore your eyes turned blue
Biology doesn't lie
Baby tell me something true

Patience for the Perfect

He never disappeared
Completely from view
He was always just there
And I always knew

They call this thing faith
I think - I'm not sure
But it felt like something
And I wanted more

So I waited with a patience
I knew not to have owned
Cos I felt his sweet presence
Right down to my bones

Heart Noir

Spent too much time
With a man
Whose heart
Was covered in coal

Blackened
The man never came
To the party as a whole

He was broken
Though I could still see
The spark in his eye

Now I've lost count
Of the number of times
He's seen me cry

Idolizing Butterflies

Two butterflies kiss
And dance
All along a clear blue sky

They weave
With each other
And never ask why

It's their stage
And their sea
Their home
And their heart

Butterfly beauty
Existence of art

Pure white as if
They were born
Of the moon

They carry no cares
Except only
To swoon

My Mother's Memories

Send me pictures
Of old pictures
Of you
When you were young

I want to see
And I didn't think to ask
I was a lost soul
In the past

I want to know you
Who you were
Before you lost faith

I want to understand
How we got to this place

I don't know why
I couldn't let you in
I was afraid
All these years
And I let the darkness win

Now it's got you too
But I've broken free
And I'm scared it'll make
A ghost out of me

I lived in my head
I lived in the past
Scared that the future
Would pass by too fast

Lost in a nightmare
Where nothing was wrong
Unable to see
What was there all along

So show me the faces
And places
Of youth
Maybe the photographs
Will uncover some truth

Maybe it will fix you
To know that I care
I know I don't show it
But I want you to share

For Robyn

The Proof

You're off the airwaves
But if I'm honest
You've been gone a while

And I don't have
The grimace I once did
Nor do I have a smile

Where did happiness go?
And what is happiness anyway?
Where did the good times go?
Who took them away
From me?

Don't I deserve to feel at ease?
How about if I beg?
What if I say please?

Can't someone tell me
Where it all went wrong?
Can I find the answers
If I write out a song?

All I know is that
Emptiness is real
I keep thinking
I'm ready to forgive
Ready to heal

Then I do it all again
I break things
With no steps to amend

People are ok
To not need me around
And it makes an audible
Awful dark sound

To recognize this
To see there this truth
I have all the mistakes
To show you for proof

The Definition of Devotion

My head is spinning
Faster than the earth
Can take her turns

My emotions
Full of kindle
Tinder glowing
As it burns

And though I know
The distance
We could travel
To the sun

I'd do it ten times over
Just to be your only one

U-Turn

Hell in a handbasket
Full of your lies
I'm going down there
Don't be so surprised

I gathered up demons
For forever
Last night

But I should have known
It would end in a fight

Worse than before
One for the ages
How do people keep
These kinds of demons
In cages

I carry mine around
They're heavy and mean
Hell in a handbasket
A sight to be seen

Now the only thing
That can save me is time
Don't wanna spend
Another trip around the sun
Being blind

When you're wasted
You waste it
Life
And all beauty

Giving up what carried you
Demons and duty

Find another light
Find another way
Find something that doesn't
Darken your days

Sigh High Fiction

He doesn't say
"You look good"
Anymore

But it's cool
That's not what you need him for

If you want to stick around
To last
Baby let go
Just let go of the past

He will still be there
In front of your face
Forget what you wanted
Get out of that place

I don't love you anymore
Did you know I did before?
I loved a ghost
I believed a lie
I'm letting you
Out of my lungs
And my life
The longest sigh

Your Love > My Demons

While my thoughts were so loud
I heard nobody's words
You were at peace
To the song of the birds

Where you could see beauty
I saw only grey
But you looked in my eyes
And promised I'd be ok

And while it is true
I've been stitched up before
You took the monsters
And showed them the door

With a knight on my arm
And a man who is sure
I don't have to face them
Alone anymore

I don't have to fake it
With you I can break down
If I need to
And sometimes
I need to

I'm grateful
You can see through

It wouldn't be wrong to judge me
But you don't seem to

Still the person who dealt
The harshest judgement
Was me
On me

I thought I deserved it
But that won't set me free
This, you helped me see

Now I see the light too
And when it starts to save me
That will be the day
I can put my guard down
I'll call you baby
And things won't seem so hard
Anymore

The Spark (that Burned Down the Village)

It's not you I'm afraid of
It's me
When I'm in your reach
I pray what I can't preach

But you can never
Ever take it back
Anything
Turn it to nothing

What you do
Is what is true
If you could see
You'd punish me

You'd strip me bare
Of all I own
You'd destroy
All I've ever known

But maybe
It would be what's best
I could rebuild
From what was left

I could start over
All anew
I never would have
Loved you

Penny

Penny is no friend of mine
She wastes herself
On smoking, on wine

On and on
Till she can't see through
The smoke that gathers up
In the room

And she wastes all her days
Dreaming of more
Sometimes it's too much
She just lays on the floor

Nobody knows
Why she's weak and small
Where once she held no cares
And showed the streets tall

She walked with the trees
Good things came in threes
So too did the bad
Till she lost all she had

Penny had nothing
And was withered to the same
She couldn't see the clean slate
For the dusty carpet of her mistakes

Couldn't see the cut
Of her own games
Even when it was over
Even when relief came..

Blue Eyes iii

The days are getting away from me
But everything seems more possible
The longer you stay with me

And at the same time
They're going slow
The winter ravages us
And coats the city in snow
We have to make the most of it
I know...

So wake me up
When summer comes around
Running through the grass
And laying on the ground
With you
Sunshine filters through

Mine and yours
The skies
And they're almost just as blue
As your eyes

Go Hard or Go Lone

I didn't come here for redemption
No, that's tomorrow's beast
Tonight I'm drinking darkness
Cos they're fresh all out of peace

I'm filling up the emptiness
With glass by evil glass
Even decked in Christmas cheer
This joy ain't bound to last

Chatter over laughing
Over me and my lone mic
I sing my songs
Like the day is long
Like darkness crowds the light

Before too long it hit me hard
The unforgiving hour
When I should have been
A ghost already
But darkness drank my powers

Crashing around
Without my eyes
I fell and laughed it off
And through my chest
I dug to my soul
Preparing for the cost

Notes to My Old Self

Don't shower when you're drunk
In fact - don't drink at all
Sit around and think
Breathe, drink tea
Believe you me
It's boring at first
But soon you'll see

It's all overrated
Most of the time
The social scene
And it bleeds you dry

You forgot about Christmas
When you drank
And you cried
It might sound cathartic
But it's no place to hide

Hope in Flight

Hope is a bird
You keep in a box
Safe and close
Buried and locked

But this bird is coloured
With a truth you can't swallow
If you let the thing go
That box will be hollow

What will be left
If you let her go?
Emptiness beckons
But the bird does not know

You sit there alone
Quivering first
To get to the peace
You must go through the worst

Hope is a bird
Who wants to fly free
To know her
Is to release her
And be rewarded
For letting such beauty
Simply be

Fleeting Existence for the Elated Insistent

I don't want to wait
For the weekend
To have a religious experience

Crucifix me
I'm broken
I'm spilling open

Candle light me
I went out
I went without

Stand at the altar
And change
Or remain the same

Stepping into
The stained glass slipper
On the stair

Then learn it was all
Just a game
Just a story
A dare

Nobody's Girl

If we sit down
To write a song together
Where would we start?

How about
With all of the ways
I'm about to break your heart

Writing a song
About writing a song
Baby all I know
How to do right
Is be so wrong

Wrong for you
But you don't know yet
Weak for me
But I try to forget

We write down our feelings
And lie through our teeth
I hope you don't find
What I keep underneath

Because I put on a show
And I smile at the world
But my heart is locked up
And I'm nobody's girl

Devil Woman

I blow it right out
The candle you gave me
Because the flicker
Is sicker
Than God when he saves me

Save me again
Take me under and then
When it's over I'll leave
With your heart on my sleeve

Devil woman
Don't play with my heart
But I like how it feels
To go back to the start

To begin again
Each time we do better
But now there are
Ten thousand hearts
On my sweater

I'm collecting, you see
Hearts aren't safe around me
I take what I like
And I never say please

I give mine to no one

Then wonder why
It hurts and it costs
Having feelings
Is no fun

Devil woman
Don't play with my heart
But I like how it feels
To go back to the start

Tibb's Eve

Are you the river
Or are you the rock
Ever changing and moving
Still hands on a clock

Stop time
Burn water
Break this here curse

And I will go back
So it won't get much worse

It's hard to see
Where you are
At any time

It's only later
That we see
We were half blind

We were there
Dancing in the summer
Hands everywhere

You wanted this
Me
And I was nearly perfect
What a perfect plot twist

What an iron in the fire

What a mess of merry men

Here on Tibb's Eve

I'll be a gentle friend

To myself

How to Survive a Love That is Not Yours

Pay attention
To where you turn
In your darkest hour

This place is home
It's the way
The sight and the sound

Find it a river
And follow it down

A thing with no arms
Cannot take you in
But your soul has a face
And it forgives every sin

So hold this love
In the most tender place
And from your own heart
Take the warmest embrace

Most people beg
For the pain of longing
To stop
But there is an art
To loving someone
You cannot have
In a way
That lifts you up

Misreading the Signs, Believing the Lies

They say sparks fly
But did you know
I have seen them land?

I thought
That the places we went
Only let me in
Because I was holding your hand

I've got spirit of my own
I didn't know
But it was there all along
I didn't need a saviour
I needed his song

And we will keep singing
In tune, or apart
Because no matter what happens
We both have my heart

Soon, Aft' the Storm

You slept through the storm
And all I wanted
Was to lay down beside you
And keep you warm

To feel you there
Holding me tight
With your hands in my hair
I know I'm alright

Because we fit
Our bodies collide in slow motion
Enough attraction
To stop a wave on the ocean
To pull the tide
All the way to the moon
Sit tight baby
I'll see you soon

I Smoke So

I watched the smoke disappear
Like the hope
I used to hold so dear

And the ash began to melt away
Washed clean from the rain
We had here today

It's not a joke
Divorce, robbery and a broken heart
Please - let me smoke

I'm easily a pack a day
Holding it up
Like you said
In a classy way

I put a black ribbon
Around everything
I want to protect
Sometimes mourning
Sometimes self-respect

These monopoly sticks
Are getting me by
Holding me together
So I'm not going to ask why

And as I light her
I ponder the land
Looking around
For an outstretched hand

You want to give up
The cigarettes and music
I'm going into both
Whether or not
It's my choosing

Apparently Transparent

The thin layer
Between my deepest emotions
And what I show to the world

I'm an open book
A truth teller
A soft-hearted ghost
And a hurricane
Of a girl

It's a contradiction
And I couldn't have made this all up
With more dramatics
If I'd written fiction

It's always something these days
Girl, you're the only one
Who can change your ways

Action, reaction
Fatal attraction
Can they tell that I'm weak?
It's a soul that I seek

Closing In

The room wrapped itself around me
And that's when the loneliness found me
Because the nothingness that touched my skin
Couldn't keep the bitterness from getting in

I want to melt into the memories
Because they're all that's left behind
No trace of what happened after
Nothing clouding up my mind

But when everything stops still
I open up, and everything spills...

Because I'm too soft
And I get real close
When I need to keep my distance
The most
And it's hard
All the reasons why
I tried to hold on
Are now things I can't find

Soulmates

Tell me your reasons
And I'll tell you my rhymes
And we'll do this
Three hundred sixty five times

Each day the same
Just a touch
Of a difference
You'll kill me with love
And I'll kill you with kisses

And it will go on
Because this is the way
Love can be lovely
If we learn how to play

Messages from the Left Ventricle

I sat out on the balcony
It's space encased
In flowers and trees
The quiet of the Plateau song
Danced in the distance
Of the cool late August breeze

I felt a silver stillness
Wash over everything I'd lost
It showed me what was left behind
This shell, and all it had cost

And though I couldn't breathe a word
No one sat beside to hear it, still
My thoughts fell silent for a time
And I heard her speak at will

My heart
The thing that had led me
So long
Without knowing why
She told me in the wisest words:
You're going to be alright

Starting Again

I didn't buy milk
And I let the dishes
Sit for days

I warmed my breakfast
On the stove
Laid on the floor
On smoky Sundays

Now I've collected
Things that are mine
I sit pretty among them
And switch water for wine

But I'll be Cinderella
Every night, when I can
I used to shake alone
About an unforgiving man

Meeting the past with peace
I will let it let me go
I'll break away and question
Everything I've ever "known"

For I am
A woman of thirty years
Learning to be on my own
Facing all my fears

Taking steps to fix what broke
Keeping cups of tears
Building bridges of hope

Ash into wine
Dust into paper
Bread crumbs and filters
And smoke over vapor

There's no loneliness
That a candle can't fix
And no medicine
That a broken woman can't mix

Your Word ≠ My Time (Anymore)

I need things to get me through
I need a whole hope of me and you

But the half life of our love is fading fast
And I'm holding onto a future
That I wanted in the past

I cave like a broken bird
Giving up on every time
You gave your word

The game gets old
And so do all the stories
That you ever told

All the lies you ever let
Escape from your lips

All the colours we lost
Because there was nothing
More black and white
Than this

Shut Up and Show Me

In chasing who I want to be
My own intentions frighten me
I run towards what I desire
But the mirror tells me
I'm a liar

I can do
But I do it all wrong
Although this is something
I've known all along

With shaking hands
And a wavering walk
I'll find my way
With actions, not talk

I learned words are worthless
Just sounds, although nice
Heroes do something
Silence is the price

To Be Love

I am the wolf cry
Under attack
I am the bullet
Hits you in the back

I am a thing
That cannot be chased
But if you do catch me
I can be replaced

Watch her with envy
And become what she is
For she can be you
But she cannot be his

Suffering is a Choice

I want to exhale
But the hits keep on coming
Where is the peace
And why is it cunning?

Evasive
Confusing
Pain here in her place
Peace plays the joker
Heartache throws down the ace

Why am I so weak?
If my pain could speak
It would howl about how
I am muddied and meek

I writhe in it all, thinking
"What's one more night?"
I'll be stronger tomorrow
Tomorrow I'll fight

Well I'm tired of fighting
I want to lay down
Nothing can hurt you
Given up on the ground

I'm done with the torture
When's it my time to shine?

Everyone seems golden
And I want to know why

So I'm burning the card deck
I surrender, I give
I give to you, pain
I am ready to live

The Kicker

In love with an idea
Of who you once were
The man who was gentle
All at once before her

The box
Where you kept your desire
Sits empty by the stairs
Marked with "burn" for the fire
And nobody cares

Where do I go from here?
What would you do?
Living with carelessness
Is better than being through...

But the pain gives me something
And this is the twist:
Is you can still use me
Then I still exist

Super Zero

I've got everybody's baggage
And mine too
It's heavier than all of theirs
And worse, it's true

They can smile
Offer advice
But they say only I can decide
Not to feel like this twice

Maybe the ones I idolize
Just hurt me
Just tell me lies

Maybe it's time for a new hero
He won't be the one we know
Out of the woodwork
Maybe he'll emerge from the wreckage
For a final show

Better yet
Maybe it will be me
Not ok
But still here to save the day
Anyway

An Expired Entity

You know I'm right here
And in a heartbeat
I could be there
But you don't care

You gave me something
I'm not getting anymore
It's true

Your heart once spoke to mine
But now with the static of time
It's not coming through

The Runner

I chased you for so long
You almost ran out of sight
But I followed you down
Because of the nights

Because of the mornings
The afternoons
We swung through the summer
And by fall I fell for you

Caught the runner
In the nick of time
He held out his hands
And I took them in mine

The slow motion story
Sped up to be real
Run into my arms
You know how I feel

Sprouting Wings

Tonight I write the letter
To say goodbye
And I'm afraid to let you go
But I feel these feathers
Growing in my spine

I undid the twine
That bound us together
For a time

And my arms
That felt weak
Are becoming wings
Because they're calling me
The wondrous things

You kept me warm
For a time
When I needed this
A stability through all the days
I will always miss